Advent Reflections
Come, Lord Jesus!

Archbishop Timothy M. Dolan

Our Sunday Visitor Publishing Division
Our Sunday Visitor, Inc.
Huntington, Indiana 46750

Contents

He who testifies to these things says,
"Surely I am coming soon."
Amen. Come, Lord Jesus!
REVELATION 22:20

Introduction

Even though Advent comes but once a year in the liturgical calendar, the older I get, the more I'm convinced that life is all about *Advent*:

- She awaits word from her physician on the results of the biopsy of the "growth" taken from her body, fearful "it" has come back.... That's *Advent*.
- He watches daily for the mail, looking for word from the university where he applied, wondering if he has been accepted.... He's in *Advent*.
- They sit helpless next to their two-year-old's bed, wondering if and when the child will regain consciousness after his fall down the basement steps.... They're in *Advent*.
- She watches CNN on the hour for the latest word from Iraq, apprehensive that sooner or later she'll get the dreaded word that he's been killed in action, and scared to tell the kids.... She's in *Advent*.
- He sits in the confessional Saturday after Saturday, wondering if anyone will ever come and experience the renewal and mercy of the Sacrament of Reconciliation.... He is in *Advent*.
- She has invited her husband to sit down and talk, realizing that their marriage is in peril, and she paces the floor asking herself if he will come back after he stormed out the door.... She's in *Advent*.

- He's exhausted from praying for a job, having begged God hour after hour, day after day, these past four months of unemployment, as he replies to the most recent want ad, knowing his savings and benefits are almost gone, reluctant to admit failure again to his wife and kids. . . . He's in *Advent*.

- She's at the end of the long line, all her belongings in two plastic garbage bags, and she is fearful that the beds will all be taken on this freezing night by the time she gets to the door of the shelter. . . . She's in *Advent*.

- It's now 3:00 a.m., and he's been the only one in the Eucharistic Chapel of Adoration since midnight, but he will not leave; he will wait until someone else shows up to pray before the Blessed Sacrament. . . . He's in *Advent*.

- He wonders if he can make it through the evening. He wants a drink so bad. It's been three months since his last one, three months of sobriety, one step at a time, and he can sense himself falling. . . . He's in *Advent*.

Waiting, longing, hoping, watching, yearning, expecting . . . seems like that's what life is all about. Life is an *Advent*.

- He kisses her gently on the forehead, as the hospice caregivers have told him it's over, and he realizes her nine years of Alzheimer's have come to the end. His waiting, and hers, is finally over.

Her *Advent* is over; his will continue, and so does ours. Pope Benedict XVI, long before he was pope, gave a series of Advent sermons as a young priest in 1965 to university students in the cathedral in Münster, Germany. He pointed out in this series that we are apt to think of Advent as a season that exists "before Christ," while we exist "after Christ." But as he says:

> It is Advent. All our answers remain fragmentary. The first thing to accept is, ever and again this reality of an enduring Advent. If we do that, we shall begin to realize that the borderline between "before Christ" and "after Christ" does not run through historical time, in an outward sense, and cannot be drawn on any map; it runs through our hearts. Insofar as we are living on a basis of selfishness, of egoism, then even today we are "before Christ." But in this time of Advent, let us ask the Lord to grant that we may live less and less "before Christ," and certainly not "after Christ" but truly with Christ and in Christ: with him who is indeed Christ yesterday, today and forever (Heb. 13:8). Amen. (*What it Means to Be a Christian*, by Joseph Ratzinger, page 40)

This little book is meant to assist you in celebrating the sacred Season of Advent with a unique focus for each of the four weeks of Advent, which hopefully will help you meditate on this reality and open yourself to Christ. If you are like me, you realize that, deep down, our need for the Lord only grows with each passing moment, as our time of waiting for His coming — our *Advent* — comes to a close.

1

The Three Comings of Christ

ADVENT

Advent means "coming" and, simply put, Advent is the season when we prepare for the coming of Christ at Christmas.

You learn an awful lot about our faith when you teach religion to children. I recall two incidents that happened to me when I was a parish priest where kids taught me something about Advent.

The first incident happened when I was visiting a class of fourth graders during the Season of Advent. I asked them, "Can any of you help me understand Advent better?"

A little girl, named Judy, raised her hand and said, "Well, Father, sure. At this time of the year, in the weeks before Christmas, I always see my mom and dad cleaning and decorating the house, cooking and baking good stuff, all to get ready for the company that's going to come visit us at Christmastime."

"So Advent," Judy went on, "is the time when we get our hearts ready for the greatest Christmas gift of all — namely, Jesus."

Now I don't think that's a bad definition at all of Advent, do you?

The second incident happened when I was teaching grade school at the parishes where I was assigned at the time. One day, I was telling them — sixth graders this time — about Advent as the time that we prepare for the coming of Christ at Christmas. "But, Father Tim," a young fellow said, "Jesus already came that first Christmas, in Bethlehem, in the stable. So how can we get ready for His coming now? He already came!"

You know, that's not a bad question either. I'd like to try my best to answer that question in this meditation by talking to you about the three comings of Christ at Christmas — the triple "Advents" of Our Lord.

CHRIST WILL COME AGAIN

We believe that Christ comes in three ways.

Yes, He has come already at Bethlehem on that first Christmas. This is the first coming of Our Lord, the one we're most familiar with and celebrate every Christmas.

He also comes to us now, every day, in such mysterious ways, as in prayer, grace, word, and sacrament. These are other ways that Our Lord comes to us. The word for the celebration of the Lord's birth, "Christmas" — literally, "Christ's Mass" — hints at that coming as well.

Then there is yet another coming. Christ will come at the end of time, as judge of the living and the dead.

So there are three comings of Jesus. Christ did come in the past, Christ does come right now, and Christ will come in the future. If you don't mind me saying it in a more poetic way, Our Lord comes to us in history, mystery, and majesty. He came in history as the Holy Infant of Bethlehem. He comes to us now in mystery — in word, sacrament, grace, and mercy.

He will come in majesty at the end of the world as judge of the living and the dead. Christ comes in history, mystery, and majesty.

This is the threefold coming of Christ that we contemplate during this blessed Season of Advent. Let's reflect on each of these comings of Christ.

HIS COMING IN HISTORY

Our Lord Jesus Christ came in history. This is, of course, the coming that drove the dreams of the faithful people of Israel, who had waited so eagerly and so long for the coming of the Messiah. What we try to do as the Church in Advent, in a small way, is to consolidate those centuries of waiting into four short weeks. And we're reminded — guess what? — that God takes His sweet old time in fulfilling His promises.

God may have promised a Savior in the Garden of Eden. You bet He did. But He was slow in following through on that sacred promise. So that's why we hear words such as "yearning," "waiting," "hoping," "watching," "longing," "looking," and "preparing" throughout this holy season. These words all become part of our Advent vocabulary at the sacred liturgy. But all that yearning, waiting, hoping, watching, longing, looking, and preparing — was it ever worth it when He finally did come, for as St. John the Evangelist records: "The Word became flesh and dwelt among us" (John 1:14). There is His coming in history.

Now, granted, there's really not all that much we can do to prepare for that first coming of Christ — His coming in history — because as a matter of fact, it has already taken place. But we can, during this Season of Advent, assume the posture of the expectant people of Israel and admit that we have a very real need for a Savior.

Did you get that?

We sure do need a Savior!

Advent is an excellent time to prepare, to renew our faith that the baby whose birth we hail at Christmas is indeed the Savior of the World, the long-awaited Messiah — the One who can save us! Now, it might sound easy to make the admission that we need a Savior, but in reality it's tough because most of us are sort of proud and feel rather self-sufficient, independent — in other words, we feel we're able to take care of ourselves. We're not beholden to anybody. We hardly need a Savior.

Yet if we are really honest with ourselves, we admit that there are certain things in our life that we just can't fix. I need help. I happen to need a Savior — and there is good news! We happen to have the best Savior ever, who was born in Bethlehem of Judea, in history, on that first Christmas Day.

What we actually mean by Christ coming in history is that at a specific time and place, God became Man and entered the human drama. This is called the Incarnation — that is, Our Lord's coming in history. Advent can be a great time to recollect our utter dependence and need for God made Man, who has broken into the history of the world, to save us.

HIS COMING IN MAJESTY

That was His coming in history. Let's jump ahead to the third coming of Christ, His coming in majesty.

I used to bring Holy Communion to a wonderful woman in the parish who was housebound because of frail health and advanced age. Her name was Rosemary. On one Friday when I gave her Holy Communion, she made her thanksgiving afterward, and for a short while we chatted, as I like to do when making my Communion calls. "Father," she said, "some pests came to the door earlier this week, thumping their Bibles, and they said to me: 'Listen, ma'am, you better be ready because

Christ is going to return soon! Christ is going to come back as judge. You'd better be ready and you better be saved.'"

I asked Rosemary, "Well, what did you say to those fellows at the door?"

"I just shushed them away," she replied. "I said, 'I'm a Catholic. I don't believe any of that stuff.'" Uh-oh! It was time for a little catechism lesson for my friend Rosemary.

I said, "Rosemary, of course we believe that the Lord is going to come again at the end of time. Don't we say at every Mass, in the memorial acclamation, 'Christ had died, Christ is risen, Christ will come again'? Don't we say every Sunday as we profess our faith in the creed, 'He will come again in glory to judge the living and the dead'"?

"Remember," I said, "right after the Our Father at Mass, that the priest says 'as we wait in joyful hope for the coming of our Savior, Jesus Christ,' and that the priest prays in the preface right before the *Sanctus* at the liturgies of Advent, 'Now we watch for the day . . . when Christ our Lord will come again in His glory.'"

I did have to admit to Rosemary that, unlike some other Christian believers, we Catholics quit, a long time ago, trying to calculate just when Christ will come again — but we sure do believe that He will.

Christ will come again in glory — that is an essential part of our faith. That's His coming in majesty. And you know what? Advent is a great time to reflect on that, to remember it, and to prepare for it.

Everything here in life, as beautiful and as wonderful as it is, is only a hint of what awaits us when Christ comes in majesty at the end of time. Nothing is permanent here, and we look forward to the day when Christ will come and usher in His everlasting reign.

Sub specie aeternitatis! I don't know if you ever heard that. It's an old classical Latin phrase to say that we view everything "under the aspect of eternity." It is a way of looking at what I'm doing right now and asking:

- Is this going to help me get to heaven, or is this going to hurt my chances?
- Is this going to assist my salvation, or is this going to hurt it?
- How will this appear on the day when Christ returns in majesty to be the judge of the living and the dead?

Then we make our choices based on what is going to have the best "eternal" consequence for us.

Beginning to look at our lives *sub specie aeternitatis* during Advent, as a way of preparing for the Final Coming of Christ, is an excellent practice for the spiritual life — one that, hopefully, we'll continue the rest of the year.

Keep in mind how different that coming of Christ in majesty at the end of the world is going to be different from His first coming in history when He arrived as a helpless baby. When He comes in majesty, He's going to come as the Omnipotent Judge. When He came in history, He was acknowledged only by Mary, Joseph, some shepherds, and the Magi. When He comes in majesty, all creation will bow down in homage. When He came in history, the angels announced peace on earth. When He comes in majesty, those same angels will divide all creatures for eternal reckoning.

So there are two of the three comings of Christ — He came in history and He will come in majesty. Now let's reflect on the coming of Christ in mystery. This is the coming that's most pertinent to us, because it comes between His coming in history and His coming in majesty.

HIS COMING IN MYSTERY

Let me share with you an incident from my life that maybe will help us appreciate this coming of Christ in mystery. I really love — I confess — I really love getting Christmas cards. I enjoy sending them. During the Season of Advent, I spend a lot of time doing it. It just provides what I think is a providential opportunity to keep in touch with cherished friends, and I sure look forward to getting them.

Well, a couple of years ago I got a Christmas card with a letter inside that really moved me. I've kept it to this day, and I usually reread it every Advent. It was from a young fellow that I had really gotten to know well in one of the parishes where I had been assigned. He was at that time in his early years of college, and he used to often come by to visit me in the rectory. I was so impressed with his thirst for religion, with his hunger for the faith, with his desire to just find the Lord and discover what the Lord was asking him to do. He was a man on a real religious odyssey.

I left the parish, was reassigned to another place, and lost contact with him. So some years later, was I ever happy when I got this Christmas card from him, because it allowed me to rekindle our friendship.

In the letter inside his Christmas card to me he wrote:

Dear Fr. Tim,

I know it's been years since I've caught up with you, but let me tell you what's happened. You knew me well and you knew how I was always on this religious quest. Not too long after you left the parish I went out to California. I heard there was a Carthusian monastery there, one of the strictest orders of monks, and I thought, "I'm going to go there because that is really going to quench my thirst for religion, faith, and for God."

Well, I spent a couple of months there and it didn't work. They were sure helpful, but it didn't work. The Carthusians recommended that maybe I ought to go with the Jesuits and make a 30-day retreat. So I did that. That helped, but it really didn't quench my thirst. I didn't think so, anyway.

Then I got into intense spiritual direction; it helped a little but I was still restless. Then I started to dabble in Eastern mystical religions; I thought this was the be all and end all, and that this was going to satisfy my religious hunger. I got so involved that I ended up actually going to Tibet and spending some time at a shrine, with other people who were into Eastern mystical religions, as an attempt to find and discover God's will. But after a while that didn't seem to help either. So then what I did was, I went back to California.

Father, I'm kind of embarrassed to admit that then I really got into promiscuity, drugs, and alcohol. It was just all a mess. So finally I came to my senses and I hitchhiked home. Was I ever so scared when I walked up the sidewalk, wondering, you know, I hadn't seen Mom and Dad for years. I hadn't written them. They didn't know where I was. I knocked on the door. Dad comes to the door. He looks at me. He says my name. He starts crying. He gives me a big hug. Mom runs out from the kitchen. She sees me. She starts crying. She gives me a big hug. My sister — I didn't even know she was married — she's there with my little nephew that I didn't even know I had. I'm so happy to be home.

We go sit at the table. Mom has made a great meal, probably the best I've eaten in two or three years. We're sitting there talking, conversing. I'm at home. I'm feeling at peace.

After supper I walked down the block to the parish church where I used to meet you — remember, Father? I kneel down in church and I'm starting to pray and I look up and I see the sanctuary lamp and I know that Our Lord is present in the tabernacle. I hear the door open in the back and I look and it's Monsignor, the pastor that I grew up with. He greets me. I say to him, "Monsignor, would you mind hearing my confession?"

I go to confession, I make a thanksgiving, and then it dawns on me while I'm saying my prayers there in the parish church: "Lord, I've been searching all over the world for You, and You've been here the whole time. I've been looking for You in every exotic, faraway place in the whole world, and here You are, right at home. You've been here all the time, Lord, coming to me, and I didn't recognize You."

Now, what I propose to you is that — for this young man, my friend — *that* was the coming of Christ in mystery. That day — back home in his home parish, kneeling before the Blessed Sacrament after confessing his sins to the pastor — was Christmas Day for him! Christ was reborn in his heart.

You know that we believe that Christ comes to us daily. Jesus is reborn in our lives every single day in a myriad of ways if we but recognize Him with the eyes of faith.

You also know the great tragedy of that first Christmas. The Messiah's birth went largely unnoticed. Nobody recognized Him. The world missed Him. The world passed Him by. The world ignored Him, so much so that He was actually born in a manger, in a stable. You know what? That's not just a tragedy in history. That tragedy continues now, because Christ comes to us in mystery every day and we usually miss Him!

One of the reasons for this is that Christ comes to us in a very soft, gentle, unassuming, and everyday kind of way. He comes in a prayer whispered or a smile exchanged. He comes in bread and wine changed into His very Body and Blood at Mass. He comes in His Word in the Scripture. He comes in the cry of a baby and the countless other helpless individuals who cry out for help. He comes in the meal shared or in a tear dried. He comes in worn rosary beads and in those sacred words of absolution. He comes in forgiveness exchanged and a second chance given. He comes in water poured in baptism or vows exchanged in marriage. He comes in an imperfect Church in a struggling world.

Christ comes now in mystery!

They missed Him at Bethlehem. They ignored Him at Nazareth. They misunderstood and chased Him away in Galilee. They put Him to death in Jerusalem — and we do, too. We do the same today as we miss His coming in mystery. Remember that chant of the angels to the shepherds that first Christmas in Bethlehem. The angels sang out, "For to you is born this day in the city of David a Savior, who is Christ the Lord" (Luke 2:11).

Well, my dear friends in Christ, today and every day is born a Savior, and He is Christ the Lord. It's almost become a cliché that we say, "Boy, wouldn't it be great if Christmas could continue all year?" Well, it does — because every moment, every day, Christ can be reborn in our hearts, as we recognize His coming in mystery.

Today — now — is born a Savior, for you, as Christ comes in mystery! Advent is the time to watch for His coming, and to recognize Him with faith. The problem's not that Christ is not coming. The challenge is that we don't recognize Him because we've been desensitized to His arrival, to His Advent, to His coming in our lives. Yet Christ comes in mystery day in and day out. Advent is an opportunity to re-sensitize our faith so that we're able to sense His coming in the very plain, ordinary ways of life and in the mysteries of our faith.

CHRIST'S THREEFOLD COMING

So there you have Our Lord's threefold coming. The Lord came to us in history, as the Holy Infant of Bethlehem. He comes to us now in mystery, and He will come at the end of time in majesty.

During this first week of the Advent season, think about the three comings of Christ.

- Is your faith such that you feel you need to renew the Lord's historical coming, to be renewed in the reality of His Incarnation and what that means to you? Then spend this season preparing for the coming of Christ in history, thinking about the reality that you need a Savior and that God has answered His sacred promise.
- Perhaps you have not been living your life *sub specie aeternitatis,* "under the aspect of eternity," with a focus on how your actions will have repercussions for all eternity, and that you need to prepare for the coming of Christ in majesty. Plan to celebrate the Sacrament of Penance and Reconciliation with a firm commitment to reform your life and to live "under the aspect of eternity," with your eyes focused on the coming of Christ in majesty.
- Have you stopped finding Christ in the present? Seek Him out. Spend time in Eucharistic adoration, attending daily Mass, doing acts of charity, and expect to experience His coming in mystery.

You're ready now to use Advent to think about the triple coming of Christ in history, mystery, and majesty.

Come, Lord Jesus!

There is a beautiful traditional prayer for the Season of Advent. It is a prayer that is found in the New Testament and in an ancient document of the early Church called the *Didache*. It is a simple prayer, but one that can be prayed anytime:

"Come, Lord Jesus!"

Repeat this prayer often during this Season of Advent and you will recognize with the eyes of faith that, in praying it sincerely, Our Lord has already answered it, will answer it, and will answer it again.

"Amen. Come, Lord Jesus!" (Revelation 22:20).

II

THE SECOND WEEK OF ADVENT

St. John the Baptist

THE PATRON SAINT OF ADVENT

I realize that Advent doesn't really have a patron saint, but if this season of the Church's year did, it surely would be St. John the Baptist. I'd like to focus on him for this second Advent meditation.

We really don't have much choice but to take St. John the Baptist very, very seriously. You know why? Jesus himself stated, "Truly, I say to you, among those born of women there has risen no one greater than John the Baptist" (Matthew 11:11). You can't get a better seal of approval than that, from the Son of God himself!

How about a little Catholic trivia here? In our Church calendar, we celebrate the birthdays, the nativities, of only three people. Can you name them? (Imagine some *Jeopardy* music in the background.)

What are the three birthdays of people that we celebrate in the Catholic calendar? Time's up!

The first one you know, because the Season of Advent is preparing for it, Our Blessed Lord's birthday, which is celebrated on Christmas, of course. Then there is the one that takes place nine months after the solemnity of her Immaculate Conception (which is the celebration of the conception of Our

Blessed Mother — you know that, right?), on September 8, the celebration of the birth of Mary.

Who is the third person? It's St. John the Baptist. His birth is celebrated every year on June 24. Why do I bring this up? Because it points out that the Church ranks St. John the Baptist right up there with Our Lord and His Blessed Mother. That's how important he is, and there is never a time in the Church year that we contemplate him with more vigor than during this blessed Season of Advent.

THE PARENTS OF THE BAPTIST

St. John the Baptist always shows up in the Gospel on the Second Sunday of Advent, and he's very often there on the Third Sunday of Advent as well. We classically call him the last of the Old Testament prophets. He's the one honored to continue the work of those towering prophets such as Jeremiah, Ezekiel, and Isaiah. His work, like theirs, is preparing the people for God's definitive intervention in history through the arrival of the Messiah.

Let's not ignore the parents of St. John the Baptist. You know who they were: Sts. Elizabeth and Zechariah. I love those two. They were part of Our Lord's extended family, because the Gospel of Luke tells us that St. Elizabeth was a kinswoman of Our Blessed Lady.

Our Lord was raised in a human family. We shouldn't forget that. As a matter of fact, St. Matthew the Evangelist gives us the genealogy of Christ — and by the way, if you think your Thanksgiving and Christmas family gatherings have some real characters, you've got nothing over Our Lord's ancestors, which you find out if you take a close look at that genealogy.

This season between Thanksgiving and New Year's Day traditionally brings families together, so it's a good time to think about Our Lord's family. There are Sts. Joachim and

Anne, the parents of Our Blessed Lady; Jacob, the father of St. Joseph; and Sts. Elizabeth and Zechariah, the parents of the Baptist — all part of the extended family of Jesus.

I'm very inspired by the steadfast faith of Sts. Elizabeth and Zechariah. You see, usually when we want an example of persevering in prayer, keeping our hope up when it seems as if God isn't paying much attention to us, whom do we think of? Well, we might think of St. Monica, who prayed for decades for the conversion of her son, St. Augustine. We might think of St. Jude, whom we venerate as the patron saint of impossible causes. But how about, when you find yourself in that type of situation, thinking about Sts. Elizabeth and Zechariah?

Elizabeth and Zechariah personify the patient waiting of faithful, God-believing people. All they wanted was a baby, which was for them a singular sign of God's favor, but their prayers had not been answered. Now really advanced in age, when they had almost given up, when their patience and perseverance seemed to be at an end, they were rewarded with a gift, with the gift of a child. And what a child he would be — St. John the Baptist. So I'm recommending to those of you who have been praying for a special intention for a long, long time, who might be tempted to give up and wonder if God is paying any attention, that you be inspired this Advent by the example of Sts. Elizabeth and Zechariah, who never gave up hope, and whose perseverance and trust were finally rewarded with the birth of their son, John.

Now let's go to St. John the Baptist. I recommend that this Advent we hold up St. John the Baptist as a kind of patron saint of this holy season. We can look to him to teach us four great lessons.

St. John the Baptist can teach us:

- Humility

- Repentance
- How to be Christ-centered
- The Power of Integrity

These are the four lessons that St. John the Baptist can help us understand and appropriate during this Season of Advent. Let's take a look at each of them.

HUMILITY

First, John the Baptist teaches us humility. What does St. John the Baptist say with reference to Jesus? He says:

> "He must increase, but I must decrease." (John 3:30)

That's what John the Baptist claims, speaking of Jesus. Have you ever heard a better definition of humility than that? "I," John the Baptist speaking of himself, "must decrease," and "he," Our Lord, "must increase." What a splendid definition of humility.

Want a couple of other sayings of John the Baptist to show what a humble man he was? What else did he say about Our Lord? John says:

> "I baptize with water; but among you stands one whom you do not know, even he who comes after me, the thong of whose sandal I am not worthy to untie." (John 1:26-27)

> "I need to be baptized by you, and do you come to me?" (Matthew 3:14)

What a humble man! No wonder Jesus cherished him so much, because humility is the favorite virtue of Our Lord, who, of course, is Humility Incarnate, as He, to quote St. Paul, who, though he was in the form of God, did not count equality with God a thing to be grasped, but emptied himself, taking the form of a servant, being born in the likeness of men. (Philippians 2:6-7)

There's Humility Incarnate, our Lord and Savior, Jesus Christ. He came to redeem us from the effects of original sin, which was pride — the opposite of humility.

In His life, Our Lord preferred the humble: the blind beggar, the bumbling apostles, His humble mother. He preferred them to the smug, the arrogant, and the proud. No wonder He called the humble John the Baptist the greatest of all!

Humility, my friends in Christ, is a virtue very, very proper to this blessed Season of Advent. We prepare for the feast of the Nativity of Christ, whom we hail as our Savior. Just to admit that I need a Savior is nothing less than a beautiful act of humility, and St. John the Baptist brilliantly exemplifies this for us. Our pride tempts us toward thinking of ourselves as independent, self-sufficient, not really counting on or needing anybody else, able to take care of ourselves, having our act together, having our life in order, having everything just so. But this isn't reality! We find that we are helpless in certain areas of our life. We know that we need divine assistance. We need salvation. And here is St. John the Baptist and our Christian faith saying, "We need Christ!" The commencement of all discipleship is admitting that we need a Savior.

REPENTANCE

Repentance, of course, flows from humility. When the Baptist began his public ministry alongside the banks of the Jordan River, his thunderous message could be summarized in that one word: repentance. Recall the prophet Isaiah — we hear a lot of readings in the Liturgy of the Word at Mass during

Advent from Isaiah — and remember how Isaiah, centuries before John the Baptist came, had exhorted the people of Israel: "In the wilderness prepare the way of the LORD, make straight in the desert a highway for our God" (Isaiah 40:3). What he meant is: Clear the road, remove the obstacles, and clear away the boulders so that the Lord's way will be made smooth and straight.

John the Baptist realized that those interior boulders are called sins, and that people had to turn away from those sins before the Messiah could enter the home of their heart. I figure that some find John the Baptist kind of quaint today, certainly eccentric — my Lord, he's eccentric — wearing camel-hair garments and eating locusts and living out in the desert. But what makes John the Baptist especially eccentric to us today is this constant summons to repentance. It's almost as though we enlightened contemporaries would like to take John aside and say, "John, listen. Let me bring you up to date. Your call to repentance, that may have gone places 2,000 years ago, but sin is out of vogue now, John. You've got to affirm the people now. You've got to tell them how good they are. You have to be nice, John. You see, the philosophy today is: I'm okay, you're okay. There's no need for repentance today, John, because there's no sin."

Oh boy, if you said that to St. John the Baptist you had better run for cover, because John would tell us that today, more than ever, we need to heed his call to repentance. He knew that before we can turn to Jesus, which he was preparing the people to do, we have to turn away from sin, or Christ can't be our Savior. We've got to eliminate anything in our life that dominates us so we can welcome the *Dominus*, the Lord, the Real Ruler of our lives. You see, that's why there's kind of a penitential hint to this beautiful Season of Advent.

The color for Advent is violet, the priest's vestments are purple, and there's a somberness to the churches during the Season of Advent. We postpone the Christmas decorations until Christmas Eve itself, and instead there is a focus on the need to repent, to prepare for Christ's coming. It is fitting to approach the Sacrament of Penance sometime during this blessed Season of Advent, with a real desire to turn away from the false allurements of the world and toward Our Blessed Savior. I sometimes think that if the Baptist were here today, he'd not be wearing camel hair, but instead a purple stole; that he'd not be washing the folks in the waters of the Jordan, but instead hearing their confessions. His call to repentance is with us still, and we need to heed it, especially during this Season of Advent as we prepare for the Lord's coming!

HOW TO BE CHRIST-CENTERED

The third lesson of St. John the Baptist is how to make Christ the center of our lives. You see, John's entire ministry was captured in that one moment when he eyeballs Jesus coming out of the desert and bellows out to the crowd, pointing to Christ, "Behold, the Lamb of God, who takes away the sin of the world!" (John 1:29). That was his job description — to point out Christ. With that, his job was done. He could have retired to Sun City.

St. John the Baptist's vocation was to prepare people for the coming of the Lord Jesus, and to point Him out when at last He came. From then on, Jesus could take over. Now I ask you, doesn't that job description of John the Baptist sound familiar? Isn't that our vocation as well? Oh yes, there are the vocations of bishops and priests and deacons and religious women and men, I know, but I'm talking about all of us, all who dare to claim to be Christians — our job is to point Christ out to others, as John the Baptist did, to lead people to Him.

I remember once being at a First Holy Communion and I saw the parents of one of the new communicants beaming afterward. I went up to the dad to congratulate him, and he said to me, "Father, I just feel so happy because my role, my vocation as a parent, is to get my child closer to Christ, and today he's just taken a giant step as he received First Holy Communion." That father was a St. John the Baptist for his son! He was pointing out Christ to his son. That's what we're all to do.

There was a very powerful episode in my life, and I can remember the exact date — April 3, 1977 — when it happened. I was at a wake service, standing near the casket of the deceased person, when a man in the line of mourners walked up to pay his respects and he said to me, "Do you know this man in the casket?"

"Yes, I do."

"Well, so do I," he replied. "Bob here, in the casket, saved my life."

I was very interested. "What do you mean?" I asked.

"Well," he explained, "we've worked together for 15 years, and I always admired his joy, his upbeat attitude, and his spirit of helpfulness. You know, he'd always stick up for the underdog and he'd always be there. One time I couldn't make my house payment. It was Bob who loaned me the money. When my wife was diagnosed with cancer, it was Bob who kept asking about her, saying, 'We're praying. Don't you give up!' After my wife died, I got to drinking real bad and it was Bob who took me aside and talked sense into me and got me to sober up for the sake of my kids. I just love this guy so much."

He continued, "I finally said to him one day, 'Bob, what makes you tick? What gives you this spirit of joy and hope and goodness to friends? What gives it?' Bob just kind of blushed and said, 'Well, I don't know. I guess it's my faith. I'm a Catholic. I'm a Christian. I love my faith. I love my religion. I guess that's what keeps me going.' And I said to him, 'Bob, could I have that?' And he said, 'Sure,' and it was Bob who introduced me to a priest. I took instructions in the Catholic faith. It was Bob who was my godfather when I was baptized. It was Bob who was my sponsor when I was confirmed. This guy saved my life and gave me faith."

Well, by that time he was crying, and by that time I was crying, because Bob, the man about whom he was speaking, happened to be my father, my dad, who had dropped dead at work at fifty-one years of age. I knew my dad took his faith seriously, but I never really thought he was a saint, and here was this guy telling me that my dad was a St. John the Baptist for him. My dad had pointed out Christ to this man who was searching. St. John the Baptist teaches us that Christ is to be the center of our lives, and that we are to point Him out to others.

THE POWER OF INTEGRITY

Finally, St. John the Baptist shows us the power of integrity. You see, John was a man of principle, conviction, and honesty. He wouldn't bend or waver, even if it cost him big-time. He didn't shrink from confronting soldiers or tax collectors or Pharisees on Jordan's bank, nor did he hesitate to tell the truth to King Herod, even if it literally cost him his head. In this era of compromise, of waffling, of lying, and of blaming others for our losses, we need the rock-like example of a man of integrity like St. John the Baptist.

Do you remember what Pope John Paul II used to say? He would say that we're called to tell the truth with love. Sometimes the greatest way we can love somebody is to tell them the truth no matter how painful it is. Do you have a St. John the Baptist in your life, somebody who loves you so much that he or she will always tell you the truth? It might be a confessor, it might be a spiritual director, or it might be a darn good friend.

One of my best friends is a priest who always speaks the truth to me — drives me crazy. For instance, you know, most people say to me, "Boy, Archbishop, are you ever looking good! You've really dropped some weight." Not this guy. He sees me and he says, "My Lord, Tim, you've put on weight. You better be careful. You better drop some pounds. I'm worried about your health."

I obviously don't pay any attention to him, but I sure am grateful for his honesty, for his integrity. He's a John the Baptist to me, and we all need one. And by the way, we can all be a John the Baptist to others, never shying away from the truth, speaking to people honestly — of course, always with loving compassion, but always saving our integrity because the best way that we can love people is by telling them the truth.

Come, Lord Jesus!

What do you think? Do you agree with me that St. John the Baptist is a very providential saint to think about during Advent? We contemplate with love and gratitude his wonderful parents, Elizabeth and Zechariah, who teach us patience — Advent patience — and perseverance, never giving up and never giving in to the temptation to discouragement that the Lord might not be listening to our prayers. And this Advent, we allow St. John the Baptist to teach us those pivotal lessons of Christian discipleship, humility and repentance, always pointing to Christ as the center of our lives and living with honesty and integrity.

Let's conclude this second week of Advent after we've prayed and meditated about St. John the Baptist, as we get ready for Christmas. We pray again:

Come, Lord Jesus.
Come, Lord Jesus.
Come, Lord Jesus, come!
St. Elizabeth and St. Zechariah, *pray for us.*
St. John the Baptist, patron saint of Advent, *pray for us.*

III

THE THIRD WEEK OF ADVENT

St. Joseph: A Man Forgotten

GUARDIAN OF THE REDEEMER

I'd like to focus on a man who is often forgotten during the Season of Advent — and he shouldn't be. He should be one of the principal characters we think of this time of year, but I'm afraid we kind of neglect him. I'm speaking of St. Joseph.

At this time of the year, with Christmas getting so close, I think we all tend to go back to our childhood, remembering Christmas past. I remember one Christmas in particular, where I guess I was seven or eight years old, and a time in our family when there was only my sister Deb and myself. My other three siblings hadn't arrived yet. It was Christmas time and I had saved up money to buy Christmas presents for Dad, Mom, and Deb. Do you know how much I had saved? A whopping sum of $1.71 — but we are talking back in the mid-1950s.

I went with Dad to the local Western Auto store. It was a great place to go Christmas shopping! I can remember I found some measuring spoons that you use in the kitchen, for Mom, and next I found some barrettes for my sister Deb. That left me with three cents — and I still had to buy Dad a Christmas present.

Obviously, I was upset. I didn't know what to do.

My dad, who had been looking at the tools or something, came over to where I was and said, "Tim, what's wrong?"

"Well, Dad, I saved up this money to buy Christmas presents and I got something for Mom and I got something for Deb, but now I don't have any money to get you a present."

I'll never forget what my dad said to me: "Tim, don't worry. You got a present for your mom; you got a present for your sister — that's a present for me. If you take care of them, I'm going to be very happy on Christmas morning."

Now, that's sort of the way St. Joseph is. He doesn't want any attention for himself. He doesn't want us to pay that much attention to him during Advent. He's happy if we give all of our attention, all of our prayers, to Jesus and to Mary. But in spite of that, let's pay attention to him in this meditation.

I suggest to you that St. Joseph can teach all of us three very viable lessons:

- The Treasure of Silence
- Actions Speak Louder Than Words
- Grace Under Pressure

Let's take a look at each of these lessons.

THE TREASURE OF SILENCE

First of all, St. Joseph teaches us the value of silence. Do we ever need that one! John Walgrave, a Cistercian monk and spiritual writer, claims, "You must keep in mind that the contemporary world presents a conspiracy against the silence that is essential for the development of the interior life." How right he is!

Our life is just filled with clutter, noise, and distractions. St. Joseph teaches us silence.

Now, let me ask you this: How many recorded words of St. Joseph do we have in the Gospel?

Do you know how many? Zero! Zip! We have absolutely no record of St. Joseph ever saying a thing! And yet, this is the man closest to Jesus. This is the man without whom the drama of our redemption could not have unfolded in the blessed way that it did. But this is a man of intense silence.

Silence is often a lot more powerful than talking. Somebody once asked St. Padre Pio, "What language does God speak?"

St. Padre Pio replied, "God speaks the language of silence."

"Be still, and know that I am God" (Psalm 46:10), the Bible teaches us.

One of the happiest occasions I have as a bishop, as you might imagine, is ordaining men deacons and priests. There's a very moving part of the ordination rite where the man to be ordained is called forward.

What does the man say when he's called forward?

Keep in mind, this is a pivotal moment of his life. This is the moment that he's been preparing for, for at least five years, probably more like eight, and here he is called forth, with everyone in the whole cathedral looking at him. His name is called out. He steps forward, and what does Holy Mother Church have him say at that very sacred moment?

Does he say, "Uh, here I am. Here are my grades, here are all the evaluations that I got in the seminary. Here are all the good things people wrote about me. Here is my curriculum vitae. Here's my résumé ..."?

No!

Do you know what the Church has him say?

"Present."

That it!

It's almost as if the Church is saying, "Words don't count. Words just don't cut it. At this sacred moment we're better off just being quiet, because silence can express so much more at times than we can with a lot of words."

I remember that dreadful day, September 11, 2001. I was coming back home, after a long day, to Our Lady of Sorrows, the parish where I was living at that time in South St. Louis. It was late at night, and as I was going into the rectory I was so happy to see our little Perpetual Eucharistic Adoration chapel jam-packed with people, praying.

As I got out of the car, I saw this woman, whom I recognized from the parish, coming toward me.

"You know, Bishop," she said, "I could stay at home and look at TV, look at the cable news, or I could come up here and look at Him in the Eucharist."

She had chosen to do the latter. She didn't want to stay at home, with all that flood of words trying to explain what was going on. She thought it would be most productive for her and for our beloved country if she simply spent time in quiet before Our Lord in the Holy Eucharist.

You probably have heard the story of St. John Vianney, the Curé of Ars. He would see this elderly man in church every day, praying, and he'd watch him. The man would just stare at the tabernacle for thirty minutes to an hour. Finally, one day, St. John Vianney was so moved that he stopped the man as he was leaving the church and asked, "What are you saying when you pray?"

The elderly man said, "I don't say anything. I just look at Him and He looks back at me."

There it is again, the value of silence.

As a parish priest, I used to bring Holy Communion to a nursing home. At this particular nursing home, I was so moved by an elderly man who used to keep company with his wife, right next to her bed. She suffered from Alzheimer's, and he told me that she hadn't spoken a word in eight years — not one!

Yet he would always be there. He would talk to her. He'd comb her hair. He'd give her some ice. He'd feed her some broth. He would visit with her. He would dress her. He'd get her up and take her for a walk in the wheelchair. Not a word for eight years. Eventually, she died, and I went to the funeral. I have never seen a man more distraught at the passing of his wife. He just kept crying and saying, "I'll miss her so! I'll miss her so!" He missed her presence.

She didn't have to say anything. He just cherished her presence. He wanted to be with her. There's the power of silence!

Remember earlier, when we talked about St. Zechariah and St. Elizabeth? Remember what Zechariah, the father of John the Baptist, said in that beautiful prayer that we call the *Benedictus*? "Through the tender mercy of our God . . . the day shall dawn upon us from on high" (Luke 1:78). You see, God's action in our lives is as gentle, as tender, as subtle, and is as everyday and as natural as the quiet of dawn each morning.

The author of the Wisdom of Solomon, in the Old Testament, seems to have been thinking of Christmas, the feast for which we are preparing, when he wrote, "For while gentle silence enveloped all things, and night in its swift course was now half gone, your all-powerful word leaped from heaven, from the royal throne" (Wisdom of Solomon 18:14-15). In silence the all-powerful Word comes to us.

Christ came to the world in silence, the silence of a Judean night. Christ redeemed the world in silence: "He was oppressed, and he was afflicted, yet he opened not his mouth; like a lamb that is led to the slaughter, and like a sheep that before its shearers is dumb, so he opened not his mouth" (Isaiah 53:7). Christ comes to our hearts now in silence.

We've got our work cut out for us, don't we? We prefer noise and clutter and distractions. I often think of St. Peter — he talked too much. He'd be the first to admit it, and in retrospect he'd probably tell us that his mouth was always getting him in trouble. Remember, at the Transfiguration, he's reduced to saying to Jesus, "Master, it is well that we are here; let us make three booths, one for you and one for Moses and one for Elijah" (Mark 9:5). And then there's that telling phrase, "For he did not know what to say, for they were exceedingly afraid" (Mark 9:6).

Silence in the face of Jesus Christ.

Are you familiar with Gerard Manley Hopkins, the famous Jesuit poet? Listen to what he wrote in his poem "The Habit of Perfection":

> ELECTED Silence, sing to me
> And beat upon my whorlèd ear,
> Pipe me to pastures still and be
> The music that I care to hear.

I'm reminded of the visit of our Holy Father, Pope Benedict XVI, to the wretched concentration camp at Auschwitz. Do you remember what he said? "At a place like this, perhaps the best word to say is nothing." Silence!

I love C. S. Lewis. This is his poem "Prayer," and in it he's speaking to the Lord:

> Master, they say that when I seem
> To be in speech with you,
> Since you make no replies, it's all a dream
> — One talker aping two.
>
> They are half right, but not as they
> Imagine; rather, I
> Seek in myself the things I meant to say,
> And lo! the wells are dry.
>
> Then, seeing me empty, you forsake

The Listener's role, and through
My dead lips breathe and into utterance wake
The thoughts I never knew.

And thus you neither need reply
Nor can; thus, while we seem
Two talking, thou art One forever, and I
No dreamer, but thy dream.

What a poetic way to express the divine preference for silence!

I wonder if during Advent we can ask whether that first Christmas could've happened the way we recall that it did without the silent waiting, without the quiet yearning of the centuries of hopeful anticipation of the people of Israel.

Zechariah, when it is announced to him by the archangel that Elizabeth is going to have a baby, is struck dumb, losing his power of speech. It's almost as though speech is completely useless in the face of the marvelous ways of God. Elizabeth herself speaks only a few words that seem to be chosen carefully, to praise God and salute her blessed kinswoman, Mary. Joseph says absolutely nothing that's recorded in the Gospel, and Mary's divine maternity is contingent upon . . . what? Her quiet, docile, humble discipleship — a stillness, a stillness captured so well by medieval and Renaissance artists, as they portray the dramatic aloneness in the silence at the moment of the Annunciation.

All of these great personalities of Advent teach us the wonder of silence, the necessity of stillness at the most pivotal moments in the economy of salvation. Then what about Our Lord? Jesus was born in silence and obscurity. He lived a quiet and hidden life for thirty years. That had to be a deliberate decision on the part of the Son of God to spend more than 90 percent of His time on earth in silence and solitude.

Jesus would often withdraw to pray in quiet during His three-year public life, even for as much as forty days. Do you remember what would happen when He would cast out Satan, as He so often did in His public ministry? Satan, of course, would always be screaming. Satan would always have an avalanche of noise and words and volume. And what would Jesus always say when He would cast out the devil? What would He say? "Be quiet," because Jesus knows Satan can't stand silence and quiet. Jesus, on the night before He died, found himself again alone in stillness and quiet, just Him and His Father — the divine preference for silence.

I can't help but believe that He must have absorbed this preference for silence from both His Heavenly Father and from His earthly foster father, St. Joseph. St. John of the Cross comments, "The Father spoke One Word," which was His Son, "and this Word He speaks always in the eternal silence and in silence it must be heard by the soul." Silence, then, is the first lesson that St. Joseph can teach during this Season of Advent.

ACTIONS SPEAK LOUDER THAN WORDS

Next, St. Joseph shows us — I don't know how else to say it — that actions speak louder than words. The significant portion of the Gospel having to do with St. Joseph comes, as you know, in the first chapter of St. Matthew's Gospel. It's here when, like Joseph in the Book of Genesis in the Old Testament, this St. Joseph of the New Testament has a dream. This dream of his involves an angel who instructs him on how he is to act: The angel says:

> "Joseph, son of David, do not fear to take Mary your wife, for that which is conceived in her is of the Holy Spirit; she will bear a son, and you shall call his name

Jesus, for he will save his people from their sins."
(Matthew 1:20-21)

What does Joseph do, after having this dream? The Gospel says that he woke up and then, in these amazingly simple words, "he did as the angel of the Lord commanded him" (Matthew 1:24).

Do you realize how profound that statement is? For Joseph, there was no debate, no second-guessing, no consultation, no hedging, no time to think about it. He hears God's will (in a dream, no less), he knows what it is, and darn it, he's going to do it.

"Actions speak louder than words," folks! Jesus is going to teach later on that "not every one who says to me, 'Lord, Lord,' shall enter the kingdom of heaven, but he who does the will of my Father who is in heaven" (Matthew 7:21). Something tells me that Jesus was thinking of His foster father, St. Joseph, when He said that.

Pope Paul VI gave us a masterful apostolic exhortation, *Evangelii Nuntiandi* (On Evangelization in the Modern World), an essential mandate for the Church. In that document, there is a line I like to quote. Pope Paul VI says, "Contemporary men and women learn more by witness than by words" (no. 41). So, words don't achieve too much; witness does.

Pope John Paul II wrote that magnificent encyclical, *Dives in Misericordiae* ("Rich in Mercy"), in which he extols the mercy, the lavish mercy, that God is willing to bestow on us and, of course, encourages us to extend to one another. I hope you've read this masterful encyclical. But this great letter on God's mercy had nowhere near the impact of teaching God's mercy as when Pope John Paul II went to visit the man who had tried to kill him in St. Peter's Square on May 13, 1981 — the man who had pumped three bullets into the pope's body:

Mehmet Ali Agca. Remember when the pope went to visit him and the two sat in a prison cell conversing at Rebibbia prison? That picture of John Paul II embracing him, praying with him, blessing him, and forgiving him taught the world more about mercy and forgiveness and reconciliation than any flow of words ever could.

A good friend of mine, named Patty, came down with multiple sclerosis. When I first heard about it, I called her and asked her how she was doing. She told me, "The local parish calls me and asks, 'How are you doing? We want you to know that we are praying for you. You are on our prayer list. We hope you're all right.' " She said she appreciated that.

Recently, when I called her again, I could tell something was wrong. I said, "Patty, what's wrong?"

Patty told me, "I don't know how to tell you this, but I'm going to the Baptist church now."

I said, "What's going on? You've been raised a Catholic. You savor your Catholic faith. You can't leave it!"

And here is what Patty told me: "Well, you know, all I got from the parish were words. My neighbors who were Baptists, they cut my grass, took me to the doctor, ran and got my medicine, shoveled the snow and began to take me to church." She said, "Those actions spoke a lot more to me than the words I was getting from the parish."

I'm not justifying what she did — believe me, I'm trying to talk her back into the Church — but I'm afraid what she says about the actions versus the words is true, isn't it? Actions speak louder than words.

I think we're all blessed with people in our lives who are just plain reliable. They do their daily tasks with duty and devotion, not a lot of words, not a lot of fanfare — they're just reliable. I've got a good priest buddy who's always looking for priests who will take on special assignments, and whenever he's asking my advice on a particular priest he'll say, "Get me a Clydesdale, not a Lipizzaner." Now, in case you don't know, a Lipizzaner is a show horse. Oh, they look good, but they couldn't pull a wagon for their lives — whereas a Clydesdale might not look the best but, boy, are they great workhorses. He wants a workhorse, see — not some flashy and showy body, but someone who is reliable, dutiful. That's St. Joseph, all right! Actions speak louder than words — a man of quiet duty and reliability.

GRACE UNDER PRESSURE

Finally, St. Joseph shows us the value of grace under pressure. Think of all the emergency situations Joseph found himself in during the brief period of his life the Scriptures reveal to us:

- His young wife is pregnant before they are married.
- She is advanced in her pregnancy when they have to travel to faraway Bethlehem.
- When it's time for the baby's birth, there is no warm room or bed for the child.
- They have to flee as refugees into Egypt because some tyrannical king wants to kill the baby.
- His twelve-year-old foster son is lost for three days, until finally they find him in the Temple.

That's a lot of pressure, a lot of crisis, a lot of emergency — but guess what? God's grace is always sufficient!

St. Bernard comments that God never gives us a challenge or a call or a duty without the sufficient grace to accomplish it. And is this ever evident in the life of St. Joseph. A simple carpenter directed by God to undertake complicated tasks for the unfolding of the greatest drama in all of human history, and His lavishing upon Joseph the grace necessary to do it — that's the lesson of St. Joseph.

I know for some of you your life seems an endless progression of one crisis to another. You wonder if you can get through another day. Think often of St. Joseph. Think of how he relied on God's grace to handle the present difficulty with firm trust and faith in God. Ask him to intercede for you, to give you that same trust and faith to handle all the pressure that life can sometimes present us. God's grace is forever sufficient.

Come, Lord Jesus!

As Christmas gets closer, let us think of St. Joseph — the man of silence whose actions speak louder than words, who shows us the power of grace under pressure. Let us pray:

Come, Lord Jesus.
Come, Lord Jesus.
Come, Lord Jesus, come!

Dear Joseph, shadow of the Eternal Father, light the pathways of life's journey. Teach us to ask with faith and await with hope the plans of Divine Love. Amen.

May we go forth in the care of St. Joseph, along the paths of God's will, in perfect trust.

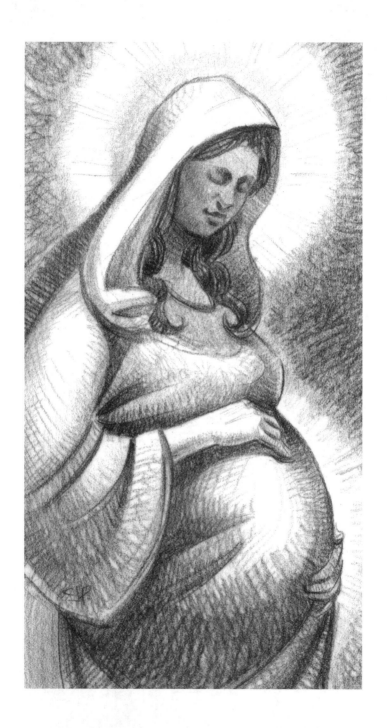

IV

THE FOURTH WEEK OF ADVENT

Our Blessed Mother Mary

INVITING OUR LADY INTO OUR LIVES

Christmas is close. St. John of the Cross wrote, "The Virgin weighed with the Word of God comes down the road, if only you would shelter her." He wrote that during Advent, as he reflected on the coming of the great feast of Christmas. Unlike those innkeepers who offered no room for the Holy Family at Bethlehem, we want to shelter Our Blessed Mother. We want to take her in; we want to have her in our homes, and in our hearts. We want her to be our Mother, too.

When you think about it, Mary is the Advent personality par excellence. She personifies all the waiting and the hoping and the longing of the people of Israel. She is a walking reminder and guarantee that God keeps His promises. Our Lady dominates Advent, and what I'd like to do is meditate upon four different aspects of her life that we see very clearly during this happy season of readiness for Christmas that we call Advent.

Every Advent season we celebrate Our Lady's Immaculate Conception — we do that on December 8, early in the Season of Advent. Then we hail her as Our Lady of Guadalupe on December 12. At least three separate times (some years, four times) during the Advent liturgies, we recall the story of her Annunciation, when the archangel Gabriel announces that God will become incarnate within her. Then we proclaim the story of her visitation to St. Elizabeth, as we get closer to Christmas. Let's take a look at each of those four occasions that we have reason to concentrate on Our Blessed Mother during this Season of Advent.

THE IMMACULATE CONCEPTION

One of my favorite Christmas jingles begins, "It's beginning to look a lot like Christmas!" If I was there with you, I would sing a few bars of it — and I know I wouldn't sound like Bing Crosby. I believe that God Our Father was humming that little tune from the moment Adam and Eve sinned in the Garden of Eden. His plan will not be sidetracked. His love will not be extinguished. His desire to save us will not be frustrated! In that moment of original sin, when all seemed dark and lost and crushed, God already foresaw restoration. He already anticipated redemption. He already had concluded "it's beginning to look a lot like Christmas!"

The first Adam had lost it. Well, we needed a Second Adam to recover it. The first Eve had succumbed to the wiles of the serpent. So then, we needed a Second Eve, who would crush the head of Satan.

God Our Father launched the drama of our salvation, to culminate in the arrival of His only-begotten Son, our Lord and Savior, Jesus Christ, as St. Paul in his letter to the Galatians tells us: "But when the time had fully come, God sent forth his Son, born of woman" (Galatians 4:4). He had this chosen daughter in mind from the moment of the Fall in the Garden of Eden, and He began His work in preparation — His work of preparation for the arrival of the Messiah. She obviously was going to have to be extraordinary! She was going to have to be special! She was going to have to be faithful and humble and trusting and strong. She'd have to be a worthy mother of His Son!

The preface for the Mass of the solemnity of the Immaculate Conception proclaims:

> You [addressing God the Father] allowed no stain of
>   Adam's sin
> to touch the Virgin Mary.
> Full of grace, she was to be a worthy mother of your Son,
> your sign of favor to the Church at its beginning,
> and the promise of its perfection as the bride of Christ,
>   radiant in beauty.
>
> Purest of virgins, she was to bring forth your Son,
> the innocent lamb who takes away our sins.
> You chose her from all women to be our advocate with
>   you
> and our pattern of holiness.

To prepare for that first Christmas, to commence the long Advent of preparation for the coming of the Christ, God Our Father envisioned this chosen daughter and willed that most fittingly she would be preserved from the original sin from which her Son would redeem us all.

Keep in mind that she was hardly spared original sin apart from Christ. As the *Catechism of the Catholic Church* reminds us:

> The "splendor of an entirely unique holiness" by which Mary is "enriched from the first instant of her conception" comes wholly from Christ: she is "redeemed, in a more exalted fashion, by reason of the merits of her Son" (*Lumen Gentium* 53, 56). (CCC 492)

She shows us in her Immaculate Conception that the salvation that her Son, Jesus Christ, accomplished was not limited by space or time — as she was saved in anticipation of His passion, death, and resurrection.

When I think about the privilege of the Immaculate Conception, it makes me think: Is there no end to the extent that God will go to save us? Is there no limit to the power and the majesty and the wisdom of His plan of salvation?" And of course, I know the answer: No, there isn't! Mary, and the privilege God gave her in her Immaculate Conception, is Exhibit A. The Immaculate Conception shows us the wonder, the power, and the extent of God's plan.

THE MESSAGE OF GUADALUPE

Four days after the solemnity of the Immaculate Conception, on December 12, the Church celebrates the feast of Our Lady of Guadalupe, a celebration so providential, so fitting to be celebrated during the Season of Advent. If you look closely at the *tilma* of Our Lady of Guadalupe, two powerful facts jump out at you.

First, you notice that the woman on the *tilma* is pregnant, as the cord around her waist shows — that was the sign of an expectant mother for the people in that culture at the time. Our Lady of Guadalupe is expecting a child — of course, no ordinary child, as she carries the Savior of the world in her womb. The Incarnation, as we're going to see, has happened. The Word has become flesh in the Blessed Virgin Mary. That's the first thing that grabs us as we contemplate the image of Our Lady of Guadalupe.

Second, what you notice is something that leads me to conclude that she's the mother of us all. This humble virgin, chosen by God the Father to be the immaculate mother of His only-begotten Son, Our Savior, belongs to all of us. As the first

Eve is our mother in the old order of sin, this second Eve, Mary, is Our Blessed Mother in the new order of grace. Why do I say this? Because at Guadalupe, if you look at the *tilma*, you notice that Our Lady appeared to St. Juan Diego as a Mexican woman, and it dawns on you that whatever color we are, whatever language we speak, whatever continent we might call home, we have a spiritual mother to call our own!

You know that a pregnant woman is a walking "Advent." Yes, at times she's radiant, she's beaming with hope and joy, and at other times she's burdened with cramps and fatigue and anxiety and impatience to have her nine months of waiting over. A pregnant woman is an icon of life itself, and in our worries and troubles that we encounter in this life, this mother, our spiritual mother, Our Blessed Mother under the title of Our Lady of Guadalupe, consoles us, just as she did St. Juan Diego. Listen to what she said to him:

> Listen! Put it into your heart, my dearest son, that the thing that disturbs you, the thing that afflicts you, is really nothing.
> Do not let your heart be disturbed.
> Am I not here, I who am your Mother?
> Are you not under my shadow and my protection?
> Am I not the Source of your joy?
> Are you not in the hollow of my mantle, in the crossing of my arms?
> Do you need anything more?
> Let nothing else worry or disturb you.

What beautiful words to hear from Our Blessed Mother at Guadalupe!

Remember, on Good Friday, when Jesus was looking down at His beloved disciple, St. John, and gave His mother, Mary, to him, and at that moment to all the disciples He loves — to all of us?

Mary represents us all. At Guadalupe, we see her so beautifully and so dramatically exhibited as the Mother of us all — not as a woman limited to Israel or the Mideast, but indeed a woman who — whatever language we speak, whatever race we claim, whatever place we call home — is our Mother. As she appeared as a mother to St. Juan Diego, so she appears to us. What a beautiful consolation during this Season of Advent!

THE ANNUNCIATION OF THE LORD

During this holy Season of Advent we hear the story of the Annunciation of Our Lord taken from St. Luke's Gospel at least three times — and when the Sunday readings are taken from Cycle B, four times. We hear it on December 8, the solemnity of the Immaculate Conception; we hear it again on December 12, for the feast of Our Lady of Guadalupe; then again on December 20; and then once every three years on the Fourth Sunday of Advent. Three to four times, we hear the story of the Annunciation! We never get tired of hearing it!

We never get tired of hearing that magnificent episode of the archangel Gabriel inviting the virgin of Nazareth to say "yes" to God's plan and design, that she become the mother of His only-begotten Son, our Lord and Savior, Jesus Christ. We never get tired of it, just as those medieval and Renaissance artists never tired of painting that scene. Art historians tell us that the Annunciation is probably the most popular scene for the artist's rendition in medieval and Renaissance Europe. So, we listen to the Gospel story of the Annunciation as if we've never heard it before. We're waiting for Our Blessed Lady to say those words: "Behold, I am the handmaid of the Lord; let it be to me according to your word" (Luke 1:38).

I once attended a Nativity pageant at one of the parishes where I was assigned, which was being performed by the schoolkids — the little kindergarteners. The teachers tried to take the language and express it in words that the kids would understand. So, instead of saying, "Let it be to me according to your word," the little girl playing the Blessed Mother shrugged and said, "Well, whatever God wants is fine with me."

Not bad! That wording portrays the humble obedience of Our Lady, too. And you know what happens with that "yes" — "the Word became flesh and dwelt among us" (John 1:14) — that is the wonder of the Incarnation. Let me ask you, with Christmas so close, do you realize the implications, the revolution, the awe of the Incarnation? I'm afraid we take it for granted. If you think about it, it's an utterly shocking doctrine.

There are two fundamental doctrines of our Catholic faith. One is the doctrine of the Holy Trinity — one God, three divine Persons: God the Father, God the Son, and God the Holy Spirit. The second pivotal doctrine of our faith is the Incarnation: that the Second Person of this Most Blessed Trinity, God the Son, the Eternal Word, took flesh — that's what "Incarnation" means — and became man, became one of us. Do you realize how bold that is? Almost every other creed on the face of the earth considers such a claim nothing less than blasphemy! That the Omnipotent Eternal God of the universe would take on flesh and become one of us is unheard of, sacrilegious, shocking! Yet, that's what Christianity teaches and believes: "the Word became flesh and dwelt among us," what we call the mystery of the Incarnation.

The Incarnation could not have happened without Our Blessed Lady. God the Father awaited the free consent of a woman before the Incarnation could occur. God needed the virgin of Nazareth to provide a human nature for His only-begotten Son and for God to become one of us so that we could never claim that God does not love us or is not close to us.

Something happened in my own life that drove home the power of the Incarnation. My wonderful little niece Shannon, when she was nine years old, was diagnosed with bone cancer. It was the worst kind of cancer. We knew there'd be surgery; we knew she might lose her leg; she might even lose her life. We knew there was going to be aggressive chemotherapy treatment; we knew that she was in for years of suffering.

Shannon, God bless her — so beautiful, so good, so innocent, her smile could light up a room — never complained or lost hope. But it was very clear at the beginning that it was going to be kind of tough for all of us to get through to her. She had cancer, we didn't. As much as we loved her and were with her, and as much as she appreciated our presence, there was something different. Her condition was different from ours.

I remember being in her hospital room at St. John's Mercy Hospital in St. Louis shortly after she had undergone an operation. She was probably thinking to herself that she was never going to be able to ride her bike again, never going to be able to play basketball, when into the room walked this husky, handsome, sixteen- or seventeen-year-old guy wearing a soccer outfit that was muddied. He was sweaty and dirty. You could tell that he had just come from the soccer field where he'd been playing. He said, "Are you Shannon Williams?"

Shannon looked up from her hospital bed and said, "Yeah."

"Nice to meet you, Shannon. I'm Vince Kennedy, and Dr. Bob came down and asked me to come up and visit you." Dr. Bob was the wonderful pediatric oncologist that took care of Shannon.

"So, you had surgery today? They took that cancerous bone out of your leg, right?"

Shannon said, "Yeah."

"Yeah, you're going to have a big scar, and you're going to be hurting for a long time."

And Shannon says, "Sort of, yeah."

With that, Vince hikes up his soccer pants and says, "Yeah, Shannon, here's my scar, right here. I had bone cancer, too, when I was nine. I had the same kind of cancer you have. Here's my scar, and I just got in from playing a pretty tough game of soccer. So, Shannon, don't give up, and don't stop hoping."

I will never forget that smile on Shannon's face when Vince Kennedy said that.

Vince Kennedy could get through to Shannon because he'd had cancer, too. He shared her condition.

That's the power of the Incarnation! See? God became one of us. We can no longer say that God is distant, or that God is aloof, because God shares our human condition; "the Word became flesh and dwelt among us."

This holy Season of Advent reminds us that God can hardly get closer to us or love us more, as we behold Him incarnate in the womb of Our Blessed Lady and as we prepare for the feast when the Savior of the world, the Son of God, is wrapped in swaddling clothes and laid in a manger. The Annunciation leads to the Incarnation and Emmanuel — God with us!

THE VISITATION

The final scene of Our Blessed Mother's life that I invite you to contemplate during these last days of Advent, before the main act of Christmas, is the tender episode of the Visitation. Remember that the archangel Gabriel has informed Mary at the Annunciation that her cousin Elizabeth — even though well advanced in age — is also expecting a baby. So what does Mary do?

Mary, forgetting her own troubles — I mean, she has big-time troubles, given that she is pregnant and not married yet — goes to visit St. Elizabeth. There's a wonderful lesson in the Visitation. For one, Mary is immediately moved to charity and concern. Do you see? She wants to go help; she wants to go serve her cousin Elizabeth in her problem pregnancy.

"*Caritas Cristi urget nos*," St. Paul wrote to the Corinthians: "The charity of Christ compels us . . ." (2 Corinthians 5:14; author's translation). And here, Our Blessed Lady is compelled, is driven, to go serve her kinswoman in need. Only moments after conceiving Christ, she goes to help somebody else. Do you see the lesson? Once we have Christ, all self-absorption, all self-concern, all selfishness vanishes, as we're burning with eager love to reach out to help others.

There is a second lesson to learn from Our Lady's visitation to St. Elizabeth. Our Blessed Mother becomes the first Christian missionary. No wonder she has been called "the Star of Evangelization" by popes. She literally brings the glad tidings, the Gospel of our salvation, personally to St. Elizabeth. She is just bursting to share the Good News that the Savior of all mankind is on His way.

What are the results of this missionary journey of Our Lady? It's explosive! It's contagious!

Elizabeth hears and rejoices. She observes that the baby in her womb, St. John the Baptist, leaped for joy at the sound of Mary's greeting. So, Elizabeth catches the Good News; John catches the spirit. The Baptist will later continue this enterprise of evangelization as he points out Christ to the whole world as the Lamb of God who takes away its sins.

It can't be stopped, this cycle of evangelization! It's explosive! It's contagious! We're just busting to share the Good News of the arrival of the Messiah. Nobody can keep Christ to himself or herself. Just ask Mary, just ask Elizabeth, just ask St.

John the Baptist — just look at the beautiful episode of the Visitation.

Christmas is so close — how can we go wrong thinking about Our Blessed Mother Mary?

In one of the most beautiful churches in the United States, the Basilica of St. Josaphat in the southern part of Milwaukee, there is an inscription on the baldacchino over the main altar, a quote from Scripture, from the Book of Revelation: *Ecce Tabernaculum Dei Cum Hominibus* ("Behold, the dwelling of God is with men" [Revelation 21:3]). We honor Our Blessed Mother because she was the dwelling place of the Lord for nine months. She literally and physically carried the Second Person of the Most Blessed Trinity in her womb. But when you think about it, we too carry the life of God within us.

I don't think we talk enough about *sanctifying grace* — the fact that the Blessed Trinity actually dwells within the heart and soul of the believer. As Our Blessed Mother carried the Divine Life within her — literally — so we carry the very life of the Blessed Trinity through sanctifying grace in the indwelling of the Holy Spirit.

Remember that after we receive Our Lord in Holy Communion, we really and truly have the presence, the life, and the nourishment of the Second Person of the Blessed Trinity in our hearts, in our souls. We carry Him there, as Our Blessed Mother carried Him in her womb.

Come, Lord Jesus!

Archbishop Fulton Sheen — who had such a tender, powerful love for Our Blessed Mother — used to say it well, when he spoke about the fact that the Incarnation of Christ our Lord continues. Just as God the Father once said to Mary in Nazareth, "Will you give My Son a human nature? Will you allow the Word to take flesh in your life?" the Lord now asks you and me that same question every day: "Will you in what you say, what you dream, what you do, what you believe, how you pray, how you live — will you give a human nature to My Son? Will you give the Word flesh in your life?" When you and I say "yes," the Incarnation continues. Then we are like Our Blessed Mother. When we do, we have Christmas every day; Christ truly comes into our midst.

Come, Lord Jesus.
Come, Lord Jesus.
Come, Lord Jesus, come!

Afterword

I hope that you've had a blessed Advent, and that you've spent some time thinking about the threefold coming of Christ; about that other holy family of Sts. Elizabeth, Zechariah, and John the Baptist; and about St. Joseph and about Our Blessed Mother. Hopefully, these meditations have helped you make this Advent an excellent time of preparation for Christ. If so, I'm confident that you're going to have a very joyful and blessed Christmas! That sure is my wish for you and your loved ones as we continually pray, "Come, Lord Jesus. Come, Lord Jesus. Come, Lord Jesus, come!"

Acknowledgments

These meditations were originally given in the beautiful Basilica of St. Josaphat in the Archdiocese of Milwaukee and filmed as a series that was televised on the Eternal Word Television Network (EWTN) during Advent 2006. Like any spoken word, they needed to be edited and modified into book form. This was done by Our Sunday Visitor to bring about the present volume you hold in your hands.

If you would like the video version, it is available from the EWTN Religious Catalog, under the title *Advent Reflections 2006 (Archbishop Timothy Dolan)*, Item # HDAVR. You can order either by phone, toll free, twenty-four hours a day, at 1-800-854-6316, or online at www.ewtnreligiouscatalogue.com.

CALLED TO BE
HOLY

ARCHBISHOP TIMOTHY M. DOLAN

OurSundayVisitor

Bringing Your Catholic Faith to Life

www.osv.com